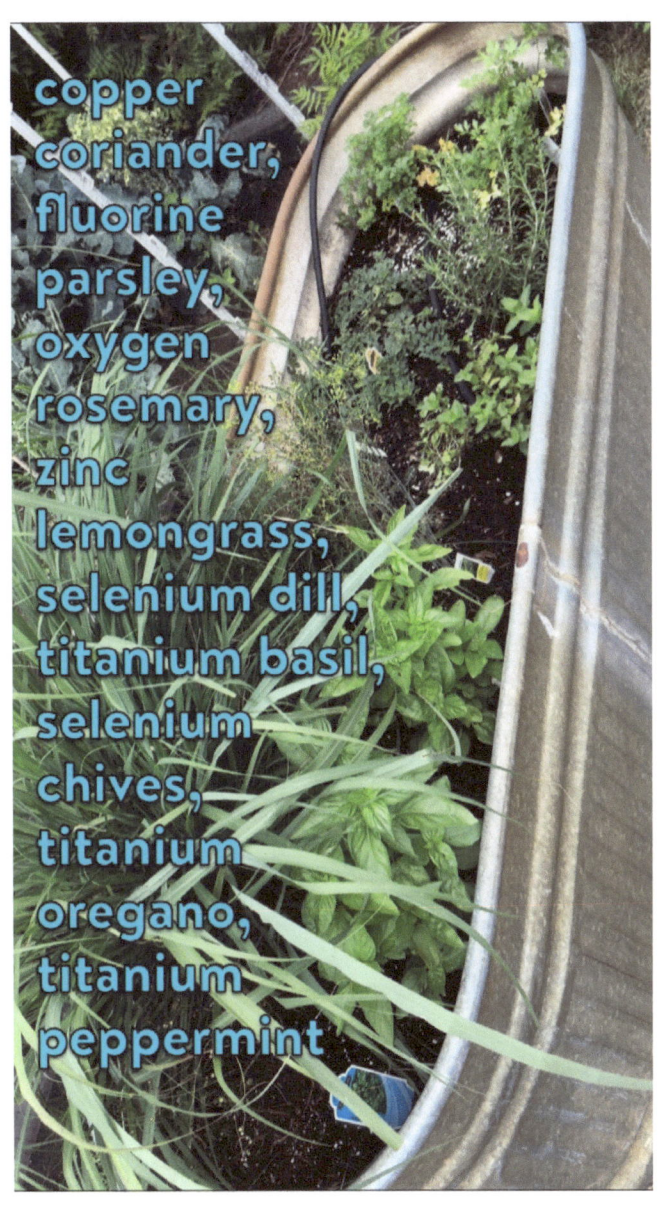

copper coriander, fluorine parsley, oxygen rosemary, zinc lemongrass, selenium dill, titanium basil, selenium chives, titanium oregano, titanium peppermint

Hello…I am Sari Grove…My husband is Joseph Grove…Our friends & family & animals & trees are called "Grove

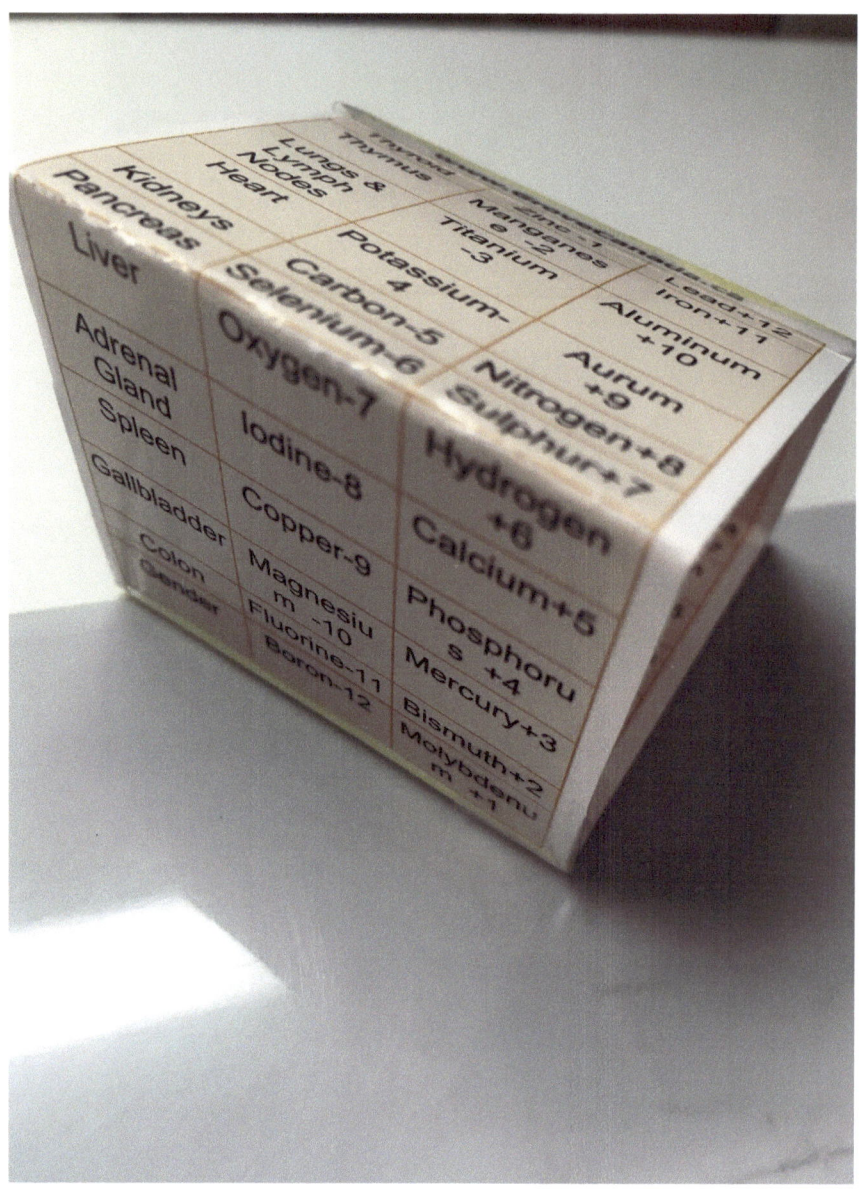

Canada"…You can find us all online as "GroveCanada"…

This book contains instructions for how to do your own diagnostic imaging…

Foppapedretti…   *Method…*   *for NIDI…*

That is called NIDI…For Non Invasive

Frontal lobe...Thyroid
Motor Cortex...Thymus
Parietal Lobe...Lungs & Lymph Nodes

Medulla Oblongata...Heart

Pons...Kidneys

Occipital Lobe...Pancreas

Cerebellum...Liver

Pituitary Gland...Adrenal Gland

Globus Palladus/Hypothalamus Spleen

Broca's/Wernicke's Area...Gallbladder

Temporal Lobe/Pineal gland...Colon

Corpus Callossum/Cerebral
Aqueduct...Prostate/Skene's Gland
www.GroveCanada.Ca

Diagnostic Imaging…

Body Part	Minus	Plus
Thyroid	Zinc -1	Lead+12
Thymus	Manganese -2	Iron+11
Lungs & Lymph Nodes	Titanium -3	Aluminum +10
Heart	Potassium -4	Aurum +9
Kidneys	Carbon-5	Nitrogen+8
Pancreas	Selenium-6	Sugar+7
Liver	Oxygen-7	Hydrogen +6
Adrenal Gland	Iodine-8	Calcium+5
Spleen	Copper-9	Phosphorus +4
Gallbladder	Magnesium -10	Mercury+3
Colon	Fluorine-11	Bismuth+2
Skene's/ Prostate	Boron-12	Molybdenum +1

Foppapedretti is the name of a Patent for an ironing board made in Italy…

I have been trying to get a patent for the method called NIDI for a long time…

Apparently ironing boards are more important to the Patent board lawyers than doing your own diagnostic imaging if you have Cancer…

Possibly because ironing is an important thing to know how to do…

Either that or, women aren't supposed to be trying to patent important new medical innovations?

Anyways…

I decided to give up for the time being on trying to file a patent, & instead, am naming this book after the Foppapedretti method of doing something, which IS already patented…

The ironing board resembles an origami fan (folding electric fan), a roommate of mine at Harvard Summer school had…

The iron was a gift to a lady who cleans my mum's home…

So I am guessing the original ideas arrived by osmosis from me anyways…

Hence, I am probably the true originator of the ironing board idea…

So, since it is already patented, I am going to use that patent for NIDI…

Because I think that Non Invasive Diagnostic Imaging is more important than a new ironing board for cleaning ladies…

Foppapedretti... *Method...* *for NIDI...*

Do you?

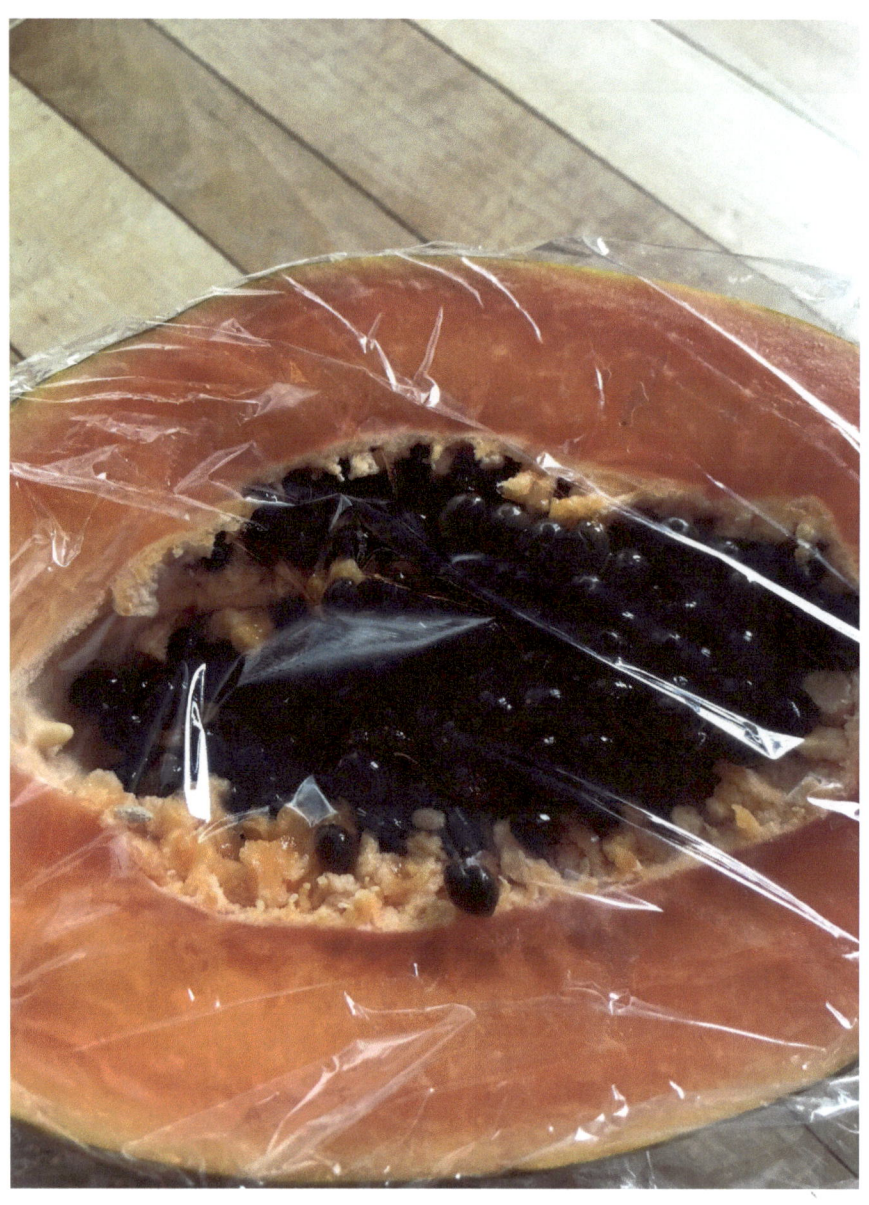

Foppapedretti... Method... for NIDI...

all nuts are manganese

Mugwort & Nutmeg are manganese

apple cider vinegar is zinc that removes Lead

You want one of each of the MINUS(detox) column if you are doing anticancer!

Pitcher Plant is Zinc

holy basil, vanilla beans, hemp seeds, white willow bark are **titanium**

hawthorne graviola, stevia, xylitol are potassium

Bloodroot is a manganese that removes Iron

CBD Oil is a Titanium that removes Aluminum (cholesterol)

B17 is oxygen that removes Hydrogen

brain parts are sided in pairs (left or right side)

or have their own name

for each part of the pair

● Coloured Circles indicate colour in Fotoflexer

The flow of elements

The FLOW Alternates between MINUS & PLUS ie: zinc lead manganese iron & so on

pancreatic enzymes, garlic, cayenne pepper are **seleniums**

apricot kernels, milk thistle, raw saffron are **Oxygens**

All OILS are CARBON

ginseng is Oxygen

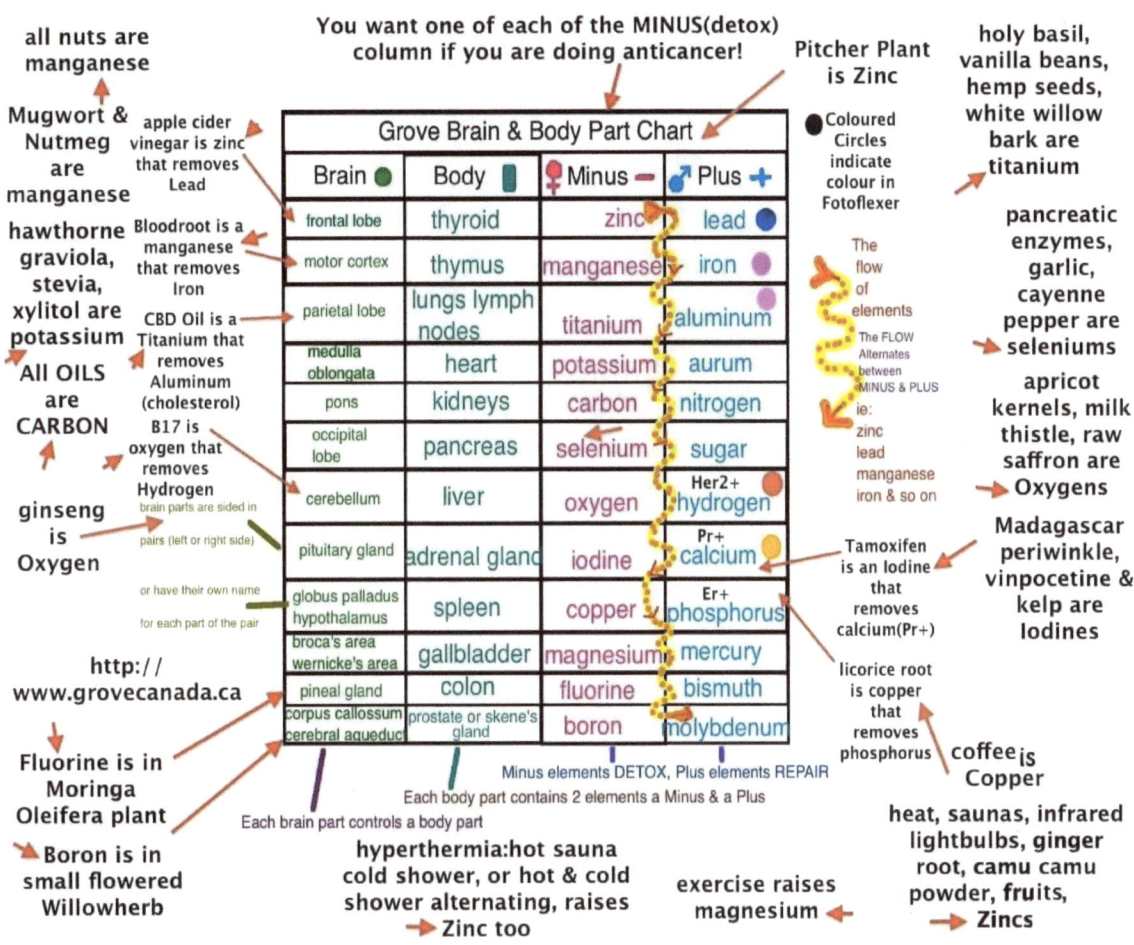

Grove Brain & Body Part Chart			
Brain ●	Body ▮	♀ Minus —	♂ Plus ✚
frontal lobe	thyroid	zinc	lead ●
motor cortex	thymus	manganese	iron ●
parietal lobe	lungs lymph nodes	titanium	aluminum ●
medulla oblongata	heart	potassium	aurum
pons	kidneys	carbon	nitrogen
occipital lobe	pancreas	selenium	sugar
cerebellum	liver	oxygen	Her2+ hydrogen ●
pituitary gland	adrenal gland	iodine	Pr+ calcium ●
globus palladus hypothalamus	spleen	copper	Er+ phosphorus
broca's area wernicke's area	gallbladder	magnesium	mercury
pineal gland	colon	fluorine	bismuth
corpus callossum cerebral aqueduct	prostate or skene's gland	boron	molybdenum

Minus elements DETOX, Plus elements REPAIR
Each body part contains 2 elements a Minus & a Plus
Each brain part controls a body part

http://www.grovecanada.ca

Fluorine is in Moringa Oleifera plant

Boron is in small flowered Willowherb

hyperthermia:hot sauna cold shower, or hot & cold shower alternating, raises ➔ Zinc too

exercise raises magnesium ◄

Tamoxifen is an Iodine that removes calcium(Pr+)

licorice root is copper that removes phosphorus

coffee is Copper

Madagascar periwinkle, vinpocetine & kelp are **Iodines**

heat, saunas, infrared lightbulbs, ginger root, camu camu powder, fruits, ➔ **Zincs**

Foppapedretti...   Method...   for NIDI...

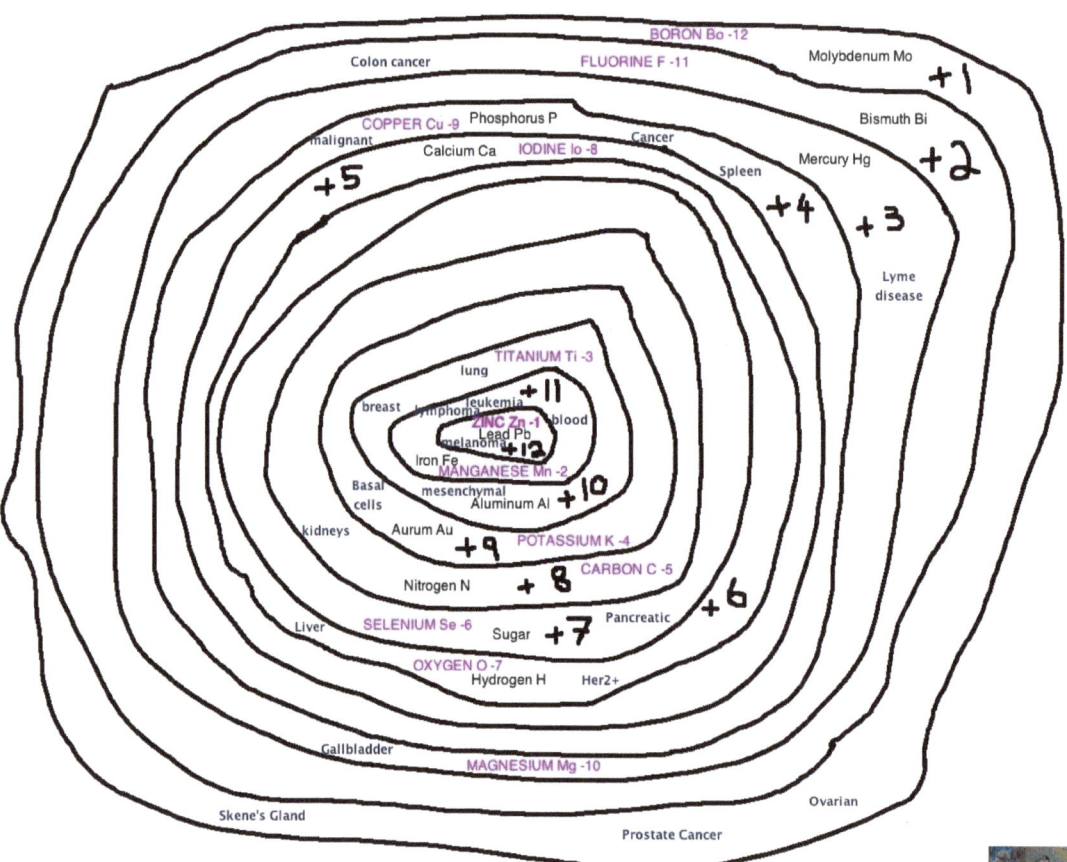

THE ORDER OF THINGS: If a tumour is made up of all 12 PLUS elements, then start your attack from the outside & work your way in...

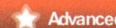
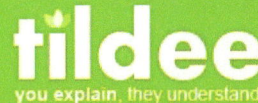
you explain, they understand

🔍 search for something here ...

> Create a new tutorial

What would you like to see ?   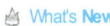 What's New   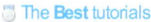 The Best tutorials

NIDI (Non Invasive Diagnostic Imaging):See the Biochemistry of a tumour, or anything else...

5 Tweet
👍 Like

0   7   ✉️ 🖨️
G+1   ➕ Share

1   Take a picture...of where the tumour is...Close up...In good light...try for no shadows at all...Just where a tumour is, nothing else...(Note: You can take a farther away picture to get an overall idea of what is happening in your body, but to see underneath the skin, you need to be very close up, in very good light)...Any camera or cellphone camera will do...Upload the picture to your computer...If you don't have a computer, & only have a mobile phone, that is ok...If you are on an iPhone, get the free Puffin app from the app store...(Mac devices cannot see Flash websites without using the Puffin browser to get there...Android devices can...)

2   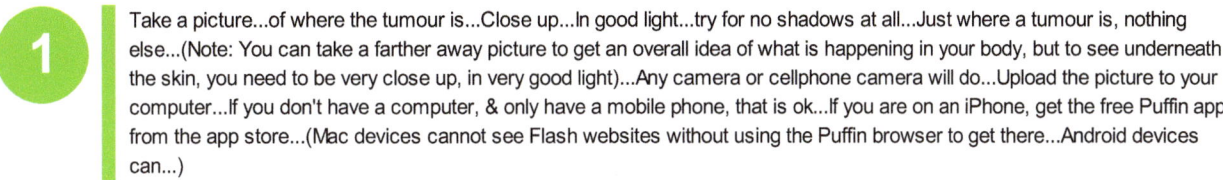   Go to http://www.fotoflexer.com...This is a Free online Photo Editor, so anyone can use it, there is no download at all...Upload your photo, by choosing the upload button...Go to BASIC, & choose the ADJUST option, as seen in the picture...

3   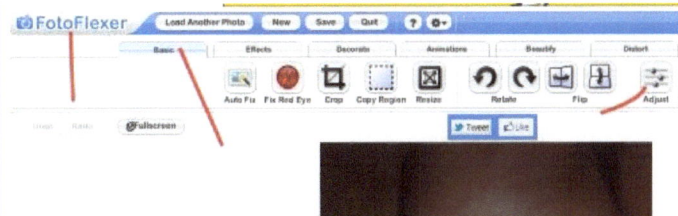   While in the ADJUST mode, SLIDE the HUE SLIDER ALL THE WAY TO THE LEFT...Then slide the SATURATION SLIDER all the way to the RIGHT...As seen in the picture...Press DONE...(Note:ON a mobile device, instead of sliding, gently TAP the Slider to the left or right, to make it go to the end of the bar...You will have to enlarge the view a bit first to be able to do that accurately...Go slowly...)

4   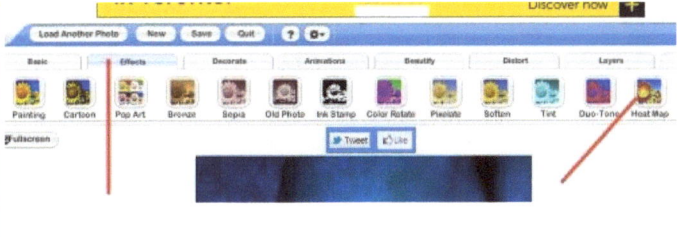   Now go to EFFECTS...A horizontal bar comes up with a whole list of choices of things you can do...Hit the MORE button at the FAR RIGHT, to get more choices...Hit the MORE button again, to get even more choices...You are looking for HEAT MAP...Choose HEAT MAP when you find it...Make sure to click DONE(or APPLY) when you are done...

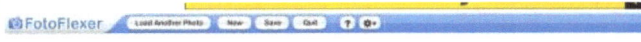   Now look for the COLOR ROTATE choice...It is

5

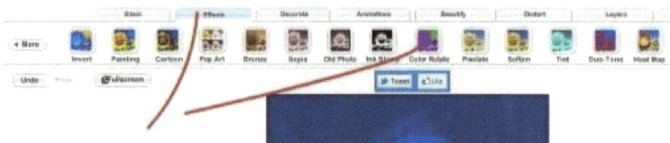

a little to the left of the heat map choice...Click COLOR ROTATE when you find it...(Make sure to click APPLY or DONE when you are done)...OK...That is ALL...You have your RESULT!

6

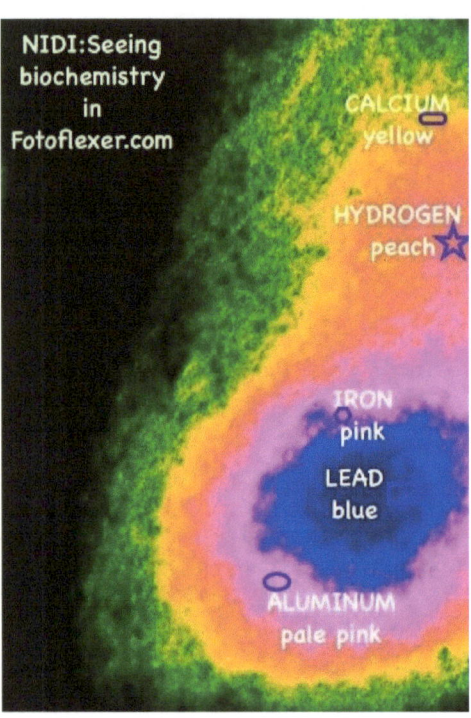

NIDI:Seeing biochemistry in Fotoflexer.com

CALCIUM yellow

HYDROGEN peach

IRON pink

LEAD blue

ALUMINUM pale pink

The picture shows what colour each element is...

Lead(can be from the heavy metal or can be from red meat or alcohol) blue,

Iron(can be from chicken or Kale or supplements) pink,

Aluminum(cholesterol) pale pink,

Hydrogen(Her2 marker) peach,

Calcium(Pr marker-can be from birth control drugs) yellow...

7

Grove Body Part Chart

The Chart in the picture shows 12 body parts...(Gender is the Prostate gland in men, & Skene's gland in women...)Each part has a MINUS element & a PLUS

Organ (12)	Minus F Element -	Plus M Element +
Thyroid	-1 Zinc	Lead +1
Thymus	Manganese -2 e	Iron +2
Lungs & Lymph Nodes	Titanium -3	Aluminum +3
Heart	-4 Potassium	Aurum +4
Kidneys	-5 Carbon	Nitrogen +5
Pancreas	-6 Selenium	Sulphur +6
Liver	-7 Oxygen	Hydrogen +7
Adrenal Gland	Iodine -8	Calcium +8
Spleen	Copper -9	Phosphorus +9
Gallbladder	Magnesiu -10 m	Mercury +10
Colon	-11 Fluorine	Bismuth +11
Gender F or M	Boron -12	Molybdenu m +12

element...Minus detoxes, Plus repairs...Cancer is a disease of EXCESS, so too much PLUS, not enough MINUS...So CHOOSE the MINUS elements to cure your cancer...From your Results picture from the Fotoflexer edit, see what PLUS elements are present...Now look at the Chart, & choose the OPPOSITE or MINUS element that corresponds to that Plus element...For lead blue, Zinc...For pink Iron, Manganese...For pale pink Aluminum, Titanium...For peach Hydrogen, Oxygen...For yellow Calcium, Iodine...

8

Know that the elements on the Chart can represent MANY different things in the real world...

if you are low in Zinc, that could mean high dose Vitamin C, or Vitamin D3, or Ginger root, or came camp powder, or saunas, or sunshine, or hot showers, or fruit...

If you are low in Manganese, that can mean bloodroot capsules, or Mugwort herb, or Black walnut hull(any decent anti parasitic contains black walnut hull by the way), or Nuts, or Moxibustion treatment(a Japanese treatment), or Nutmeg...

If you are low in Titanium that can mean hulled hemp seeds or basil leafs or Holy Basil supplement, or Frankincense tears or incense or oil, or Mint leafs or Oregano oil, or Chamomile tea, or CBD oil(Cannabidiol), or white willow bark extract, or aspirin...

if you are low in Oxygen that can mean B17 pills, or Apricot kernels, or Dandelion greens or root, or Milk thistle, or any decent liver supplement(like Hepa plus by Usana), or a Papaya seed smoothie(papaya seeds are high in Oxygen-blend with papaya & pineapple & banana & cloves & vanilla beans & aloe drink to make the seeds taste better-this is an anti parasitic recipe too!)...

If you are low in Iodine that can mean eating Arame & other seaweeds, taking Iodoral pills(minimum 12.5 mg daily-up to 50 mg daily), Any liquid Iodine supplement, Kelp pills or liquid...)

9

Make sure that you take all the other MINUS items on the chart...One of each...

For Copper use Licorice root(1/3 cup simmer in good water 3 cups drink daily)...Also for Copper drink coffee or tea(caffeinated, & at 6 cups daily you get medicinal benefit)...Copper can also be eating coriander seeds & eating Cilantro leafs...

For Fluorine use Moringa Oleifera(can go in a smoothie)...

For Boron, a supplement is fine, or Small flowered Willowherb is Boron too...Magnesium can mean Epsom salt baths(or orally)...

Xylitol & Stevia are high in Potassium so use them in your hot drinks liberally...

Carbons are all the oils...Castor oil is great...hemp oil...Flaxseed oil...Grapeseed oil...Any oil you like...Baking soda is also a Carbon...

Selenium can mean raw garlic(chop & swallow the cloves with liquid), or Pancreatic enzymes, or Sriracha sauce(mix sriracha sauce into a little orange juice & drink fast), or onions, or cayenne pepper or any hot pepper, or black pepper, or chives & green onions, wasabi, horseradish, spicy things/tabasco...L-Lyisine is also a selenium...Selenium supplements too...

10

Since Plus elements are in EXCESS with cancer...AVOID meat(Lead), sugar, gluten(Nitrogen), dairy(Calcium, Cheeses & yogurts & kefir & cottage cheese!(Phosphorus)...

Avoid supplements containing any of the Plus elements...

so:no probiotics which are Phosphorus,

no Iron,

No B12 which is Aurum,

No Bismuth which includes melatonin,

No antipsychotics which are also Lead,

No zeolites or bentonite clay which are Aluminum,

no maple syrup or honey products which are Sugar,

Liquids are Hydrogens so be careful with them(Her2+ is a Hydrogen marker),

No birth control drugs or HRT (hormone replacement therapy drugs or naturals)which are Calcium(progesterone)-(high dose oral contraceptives also include estrogen which is a Phosphorus)...

11

There is much more information about all these ideas on my blog & in my free books which are all available at http://www.grovecanada.ca...Please join our "DIY cancer repair manual" Facebook group, for support & to ask questions...

*If you would like Sari Grove to do the editing for you, friend her first, then send a picture via the private messages service on Facebook...

12

Don't forget to learn how to do the Lunapic edit & the Pixlr edit as well! (Lunapic checks for cancer, & Pixlr helps to track size changes!)...

ps.If you have done edits yourself, & think others may benefit, please post the photos in the DIY Cancer repair manual group...https://www.facebook.com/groups/DIYCancerRepairManual/ Update your photos over time, so people can see change, & know how it is that you improved! (NIDI is relatively new, so the more documentation we have, the better it will be!)

Thanks, Sari Grove(Sari sounds like Mary)

Rating

What do you think about this tutorial ?

Comments

Other tutorials from this author

• Getting rid of a breast Cancer lump...

• A new way to understand how the human machine works...(& thus be able to repair it when things go wrong!)

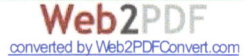

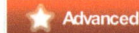
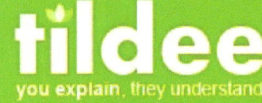
you explain, they understand

Q search for something here ...

> Create a new tutorial

What would you like to see ? 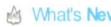 What's New The Best tutorials

NIDI(Non Invasive Diagnostic Imaging):Part 2, Seeing if there is cancer present, how much & where...(Using Lunapic.com free photo editor)

Added by GroveCanada
November 29, 2016, 6:42 pm → version: 1
Language: English
Average rating:
by 0 user
Viewed: 89 times

14 Tweet
Like
0
G+1

1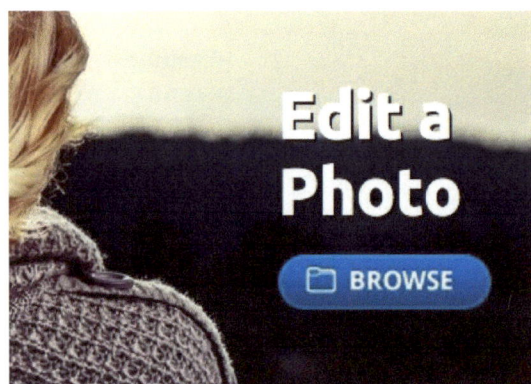

Take a picture & upload it to Lunapic.com (choose Browse, then find your pic in your computer or mobile device)...

2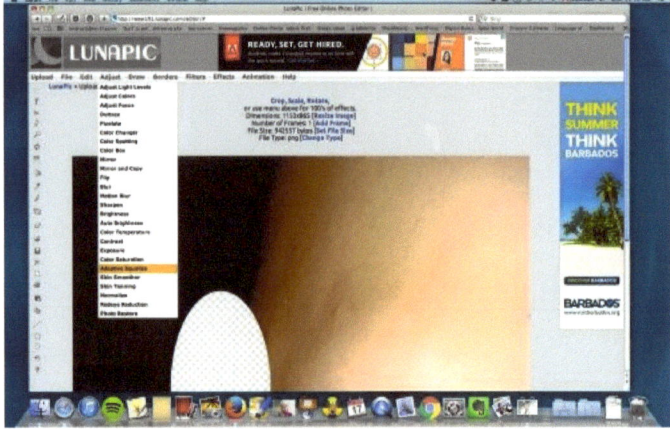

Choose Adaptive Equalize from the drop down menu called ADJUST...

3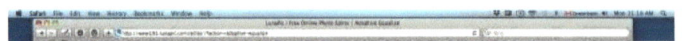

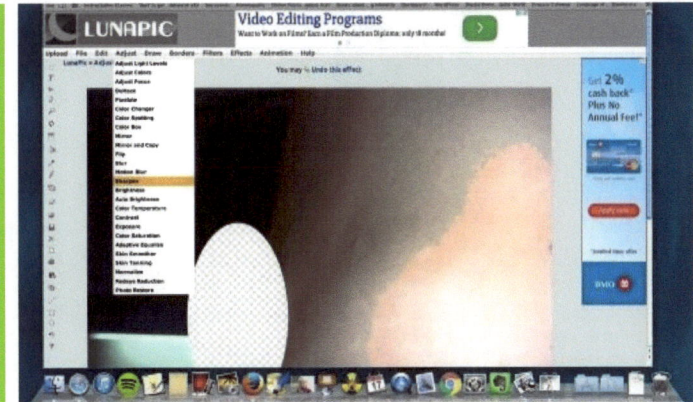

Choose Sharpen from the drop down menu called ADJUST...

4

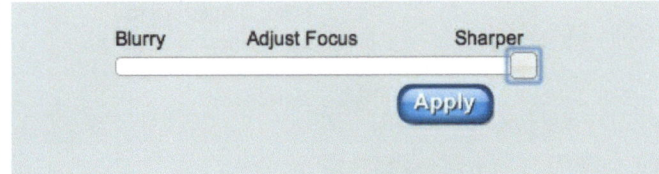

In SHARPEN slide the slider all the way to the right...On a mobile device, tap the slider at the far right to make it go there...click APPLY...

5

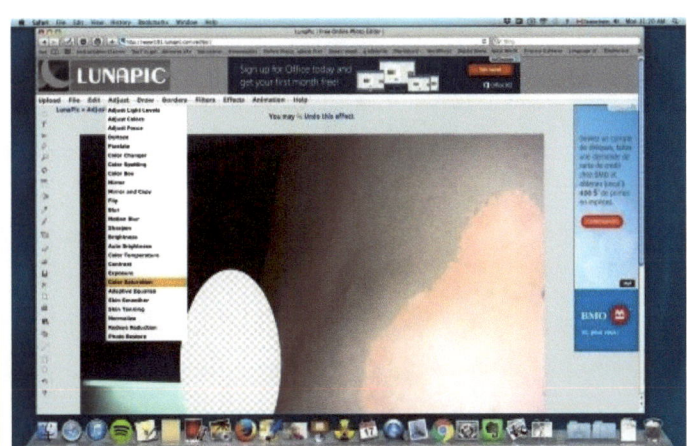

Choose COLOR SATURATION from the ADJUST menu...

6

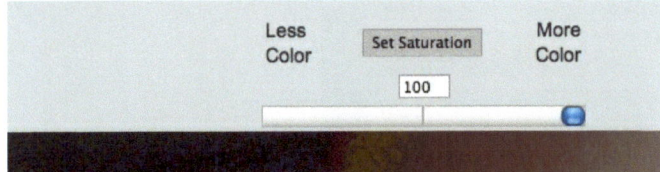

Move the slider all the way to the RIGHT...Or change the number in the box from 50 to 100...Click SET SATURATION when done...

7

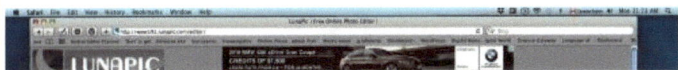

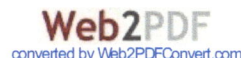

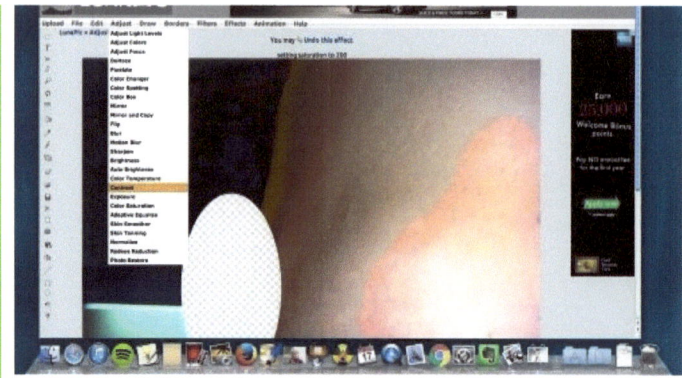

Choose CONTRAST from the ADJUST menu...

8

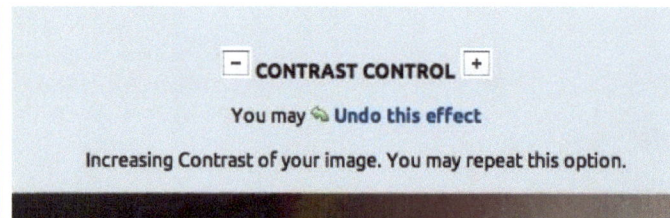

In CONTRAST, hit the + button 5 times in a row slowly...(wait for page to reload before hitting it again!!!)

9

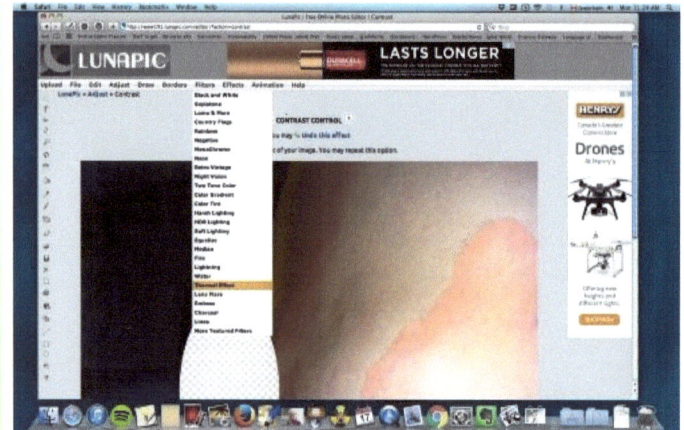

Now go to FILTERS & choose THERMAL EFFECT from the drop down Menu...

10

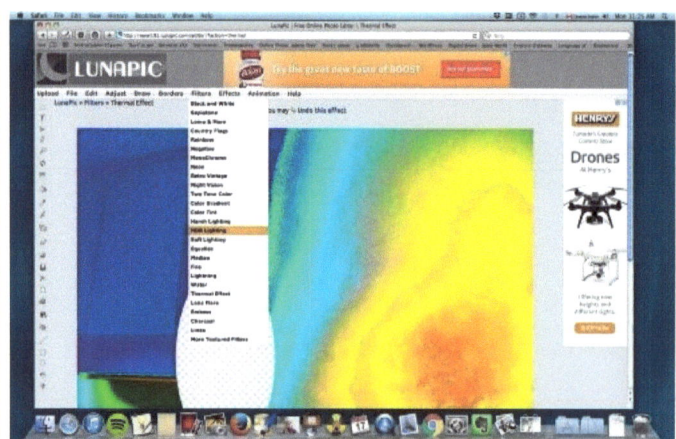

In FILTERS again, choose HDR LIGHTING from the dropdown menu...

11

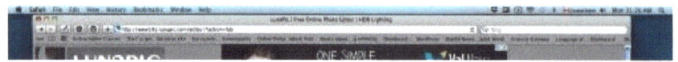

Now go

11

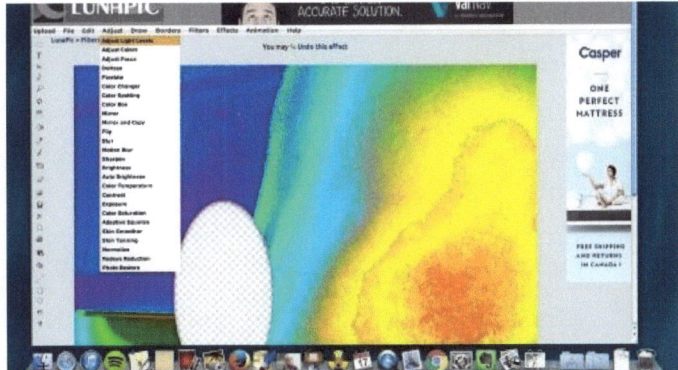

back to

ADJUST & choose the first choice which is ADJUST LIGHT LEVELS...

12

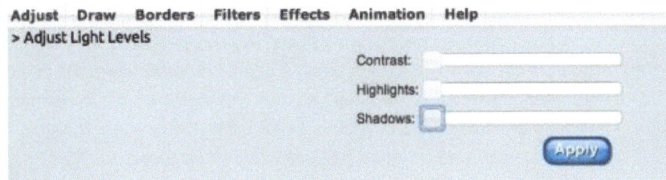

IN Adjust Light levels there are 3 sliders...Slide all three, one at a time, slowly, to the LEFT...(on a mobile device, enlarge the picture, then TAP the bar at the far LEFT to make it go there)...

So Contrast, then Highlights, then Shadows, all the way to the LEFT please...

Click APPLY when done...(don't forget!)

13

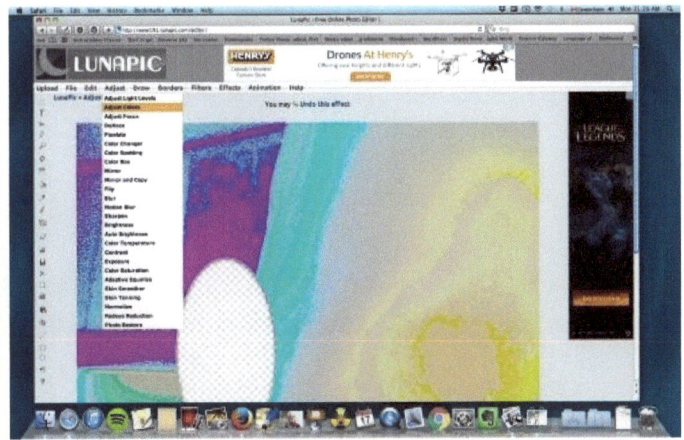

Now in Adjust again, choose the second choice which is ADJUST COLORS...

14

In Adjust Colors, you are going to click ALL THREE choices, slowly, one after another...

So click in SWAP COLORS **Red & Green, then Green & Blue, then Blue & Red...**

Click APPLY when done, don't forget!

15

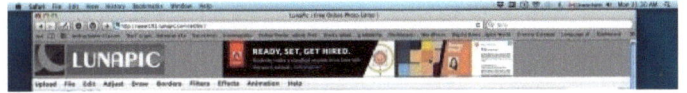

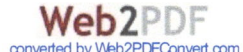

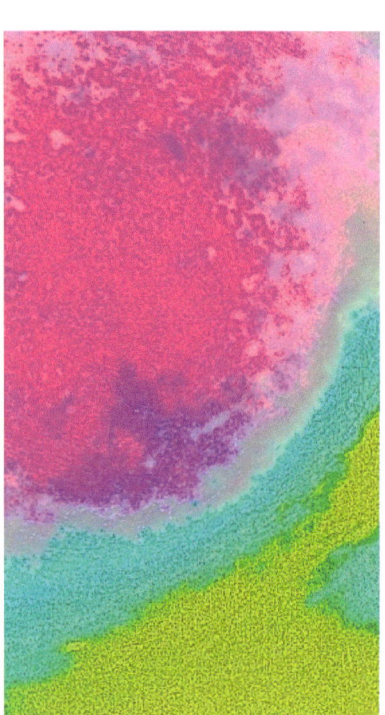

Last step!!! In ADJUST again, choose NORMALIZE...

16 The colour PURPLE in Lunapic is Phosphorus which is a Cancer marker...(not the pink!) See the purple area in this breast lump? That is where the cancer is...(a tumour is usually just a fraction cancer & the rest is nothing to worry about)...Also note:Cancer does not always sit on a tumour-sometimes it sits in a corner near to a tumour...That is normal...Don't always expect the purple to be right on a tumour area...(Very Pale purple or mauve indicates high Phosphorus levels & a pre-cancer stage...Many doctors just call this cancer too...)

17 That purple area, the Phosphorus responds well to the Copper family, which includes for example:

Eating Cilantro leafs

Eating Coriander seeds

Drinking coffee(like 6 cups a day)

Drinking tea(strong & more is better again)

Buy a bag of licorice root from a herb store online...Take 1/3 cup licorice root, simmer in 3 cups good water for 15 minutes or so, then drink daily...This will make the purple in your picture go away...You will be able to see it happen...When your lump is benign there will be no more purple in the picture...(I did this using licorice root by the way-other forms work too-capsules, tincture, just make sure it is very very strong daily...Not the dilute tea bags type of thing...This is medicine, not for taste sorry!)

Rating

What do you think about this tutorial ?

Comments

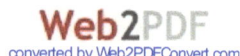

Other tutorials from this author

• Getting rid of a breast Cancer lump...

• A new way to understand how the human machine works...(& thus be able to repair it when things go wrong!)

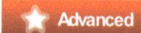
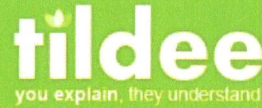
you explain, they understand

search for something here ...

> **Create a new tutorial**

What would you like to see ?   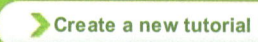 What's New   The Best tutorials

NIDI Part 3:Seeing size change(of a tumour) &/or inflammation areas & even injury areas...

Last modification by GroveCanada
December 1, 2016, 10:57 pm → version: 2
Language: English
Average rating:
by 0 user
Viewed: 9 times

0   Tweet
Like

0   0

G+1   Share

1

Take a picture with ANY camera you have including your cellphone camera...

***if you are on an iPhone or an iPad, you need to use the free PUFFIN app from the app store to access the free online photo editor you are going to use...

**If you are on an Android mobile phone you are fine...(Mac devices need Puffin to get onto flash websites)...

Go to Pixlr.com/editor & upload your picture there...(do this from PUFFIN if you are on an iPad or iPhone)!

2

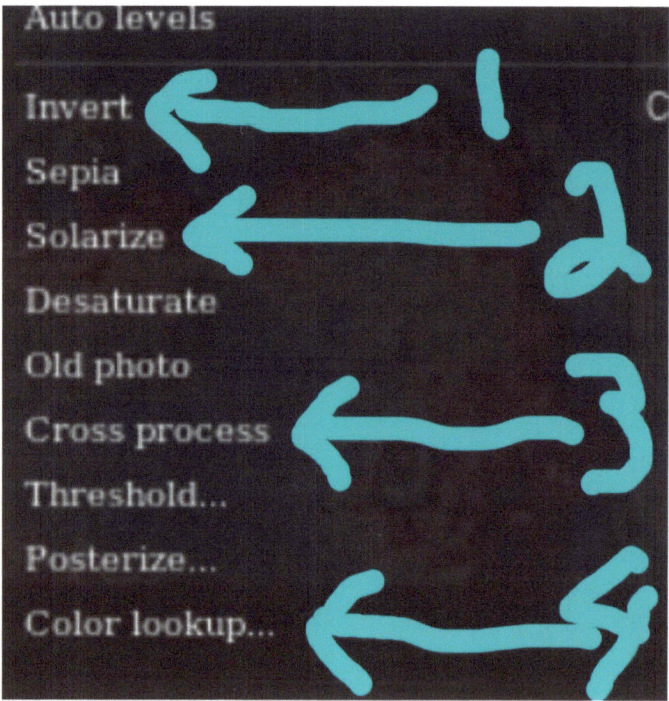

Ok...

The picture shows the 4 steps you need to do to do this edit...All 4 steps are in the Dropdown menu called ADJUSTMENT...

Step 1) INVERT

Step 2)Solarize

Step 3)Cross process

Step 4)Color Lookup ...**BY THE WAY...In COLOR LOOKUP there is an EXTRA thing you have to do...When you get to this step, go to the next tip to see what to do...**

3

●●○○○ ROGERS 🔋   4:52 PM   🔋 97% ▬▬   COLOR LookUP ...Ok, when you click on Color Lookup, underneath your photo,

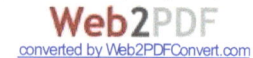

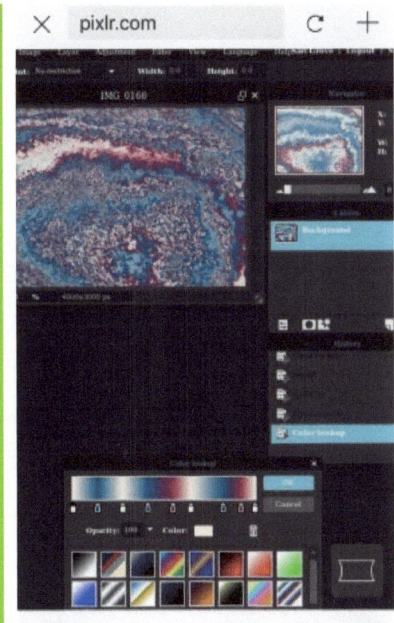

there will be a box that opens up, that has all sorts of different choices of what you can do...Scroll down the page to see your choices...Go to the next tip...

In Color lookup, in that box with choices, look for the choice I have circled in turquoise below...The red & blue box...(it's in the second row of choices on the right)...Choose that(click it)...Ok, now you are done!

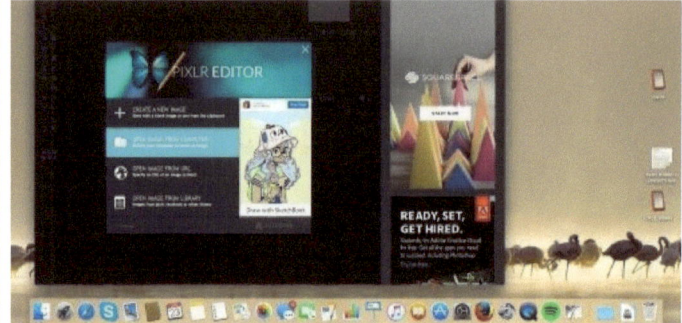

Here are the steps again, one by one, in pictures...Upload...

6

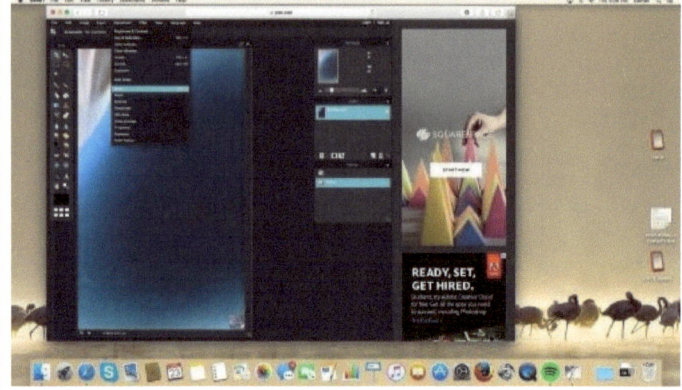

Invert...

7

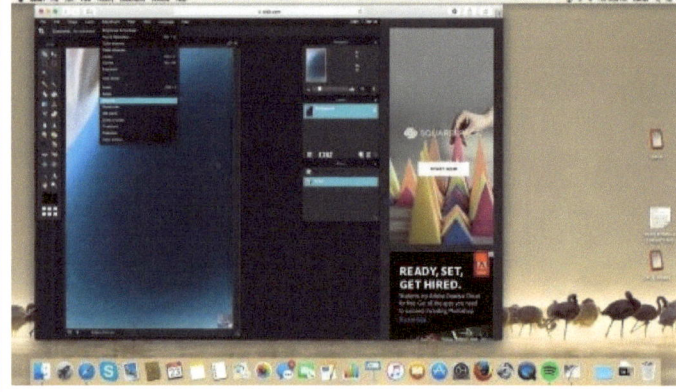

Solarize...

8

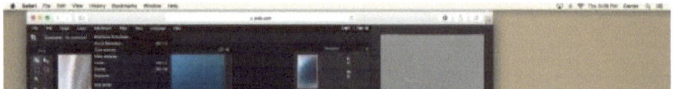

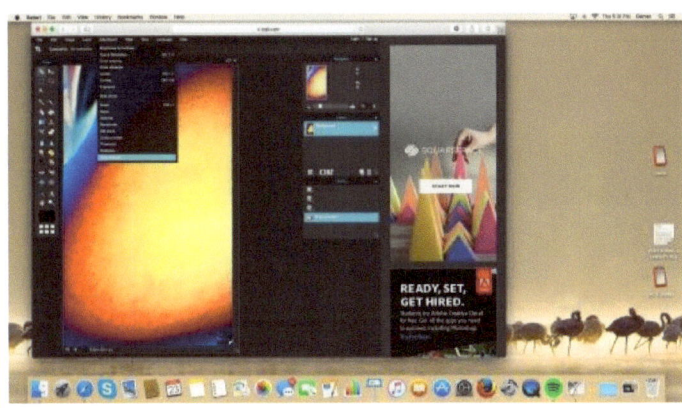

Cross process...

9

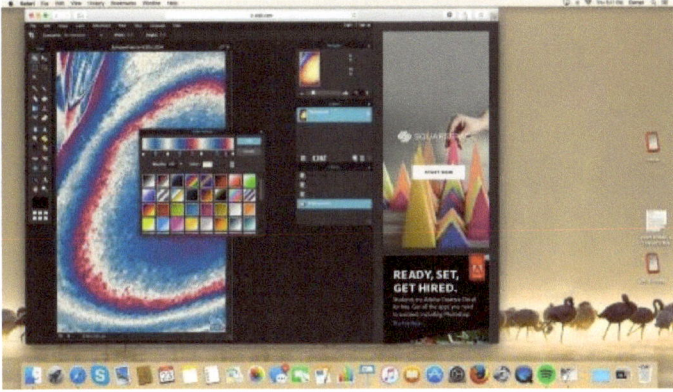

Color Lookup...

10

Color Lookup choose the red blue box in the second row at far right...(scroll down page to see popup box with choices)...

Done!

Results:The red areas will usually help to define the outer edge of where a tumour is...

This can help you to track size changes over time...

The red by the way is Hydrogen...

So if you have had an injury to an area (say you were punched in the eye), you will see red where there is swelling or inflammation...

The body attempts to heal injuries by sending in Hydrogen...(which is why when you have a surgery to remove a lump, the area will get flooded with Hydrogen, which can be dangerous if there are still cancerous cells circulating because some parasites can live on water/hydrogen(like liver flukes)...This is why people sometimes get recurrence right on surgical sites...

Remove Hydrogen with Oxygens...B17 pills, apricot kernels, Papaya seeds, milk thistle, outdoor fresh air exercise for a long time, dandelion root, burdock root, seeds of citrus fruits(peel too), modified citrus pectin supplements...Cancer hates Oxygen so go big time on the Oxygens...Daily hours of far outdoor fresh air walking is my favourite way to get Oxygen...

ps...Don't drown your body with Hydrogen if you have cancer/parasites/worms...That means put away the gallons of water notion for the time being...Many parasites get killed by just dehydrating them...Go dry...(that means no alcohol too sorry)...

Rating

What do you think about this tutorial ?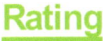

Comments

Other tutorials from this author

- Getting rid of a breast Cancer lump...

- A new way to understand how the human machine works...(& thus be able to repair it when things go wrong!)

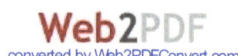

Toronto Area health Centres... Minus element for Women   Non-dominant Male element

St Joseph's Health	Zn -1	Zinc	
Womens college	Mn-2	Manganese	
Mount Sinai Hospital	Ti-3	Titanium	
North York General	K-4	Potassium	
Toronto General Hospital	C-5	Carbon	
Baycrest Centre for rehabilitation	Se-6	Selenium	
St.Michael's Hospital	O-7	Oxygen	
Sunnybrook Health Centre	Io-8	Iodine	
Sick Children's Hospital	Cu-9	Copper	
Cleveland Clinic	Mg-10	Magnesium	
Princess Margaret	F-11	Fluorine	
Scarborough General	Bo-12	Boron	

Common Correlations:

Hydrogen H +6 & Sugar +7...Alcohol

Calcium Ca +5 & Molybdenum Mb +1...Contraceptives

Lead Pb +12 & Nitrogen N +8...WaterPipes

Flow:

Plus elements flow down...(though body part opposite is included)!

Minus elements flow up...(though body part opposite is included)!

Chart zig zags from Minus to Plus starting with Zinc...(Zinc,Lead, then Manganese, Iron)...

Prevention is Above, Cure is below...ie: If you drink too much caffeinated coffee Cu Copper -9, then you can cure the panic feelings by eating say a piece of gruyere Cheese P Phosphorus +4...or you can prevent the panic feeling beforehand, by loading up on lactose intolerant milk Ca calcium +5...

Women are Minus element dominant, Plus element Non-dominant... Men are Minus element Non-dominant, Plus element dominant... Cancer is a disease of Excess...Which means too many Plus elements...Not enough Minus elements...

Which is why we need more women, Minus element dominant doctors, in Ontario!

The chart is a basic understanding of Health care centres in the Ontario area (Canada, Toronto-ish), & what Minus element you might be given where...

Alternative or Do It Yourself medicine types can copy or mimic these ideas themselves...

For example:

Grapefruit=Zinc Zn-1
Almonds=Manganese Mn-2
Chamomile=Titanium Ti-3
Banana peel=Potassium K-4
Oil=Carbon C-5
Garlic=Selenium Se-6
Papaya seeds=Oxygen O-7
Seaweed=Iodine Io-8
Coffee=Copper Cu-9
Exercise=Magnesium Mg-10
Toothpaste=Fluorine F-11
Celery=Boron Bo-12

When you get your results in NIDI, use this chart to assume that another element is also present…

NIDI Non Invasive diagnostic imaging

Lead	Blue in Fotoflexer
Iron	Pink Fotoflexer
Aluminum	Pale Pink Fotoflexer
Aurum	Purple Lunapic
Nitrogen	Yellow Fotoflexer
Sugar	Red Pixlr
Hydrogen	Red Pixlr
Calcium	Yellow Fotoflexer
Phosphorus	Purple Lunapic
Mercury	Pale Pink Fotoflexer
Bismuth	Key Lime Lunapic
Molybdenum	Blue Fotoflexer

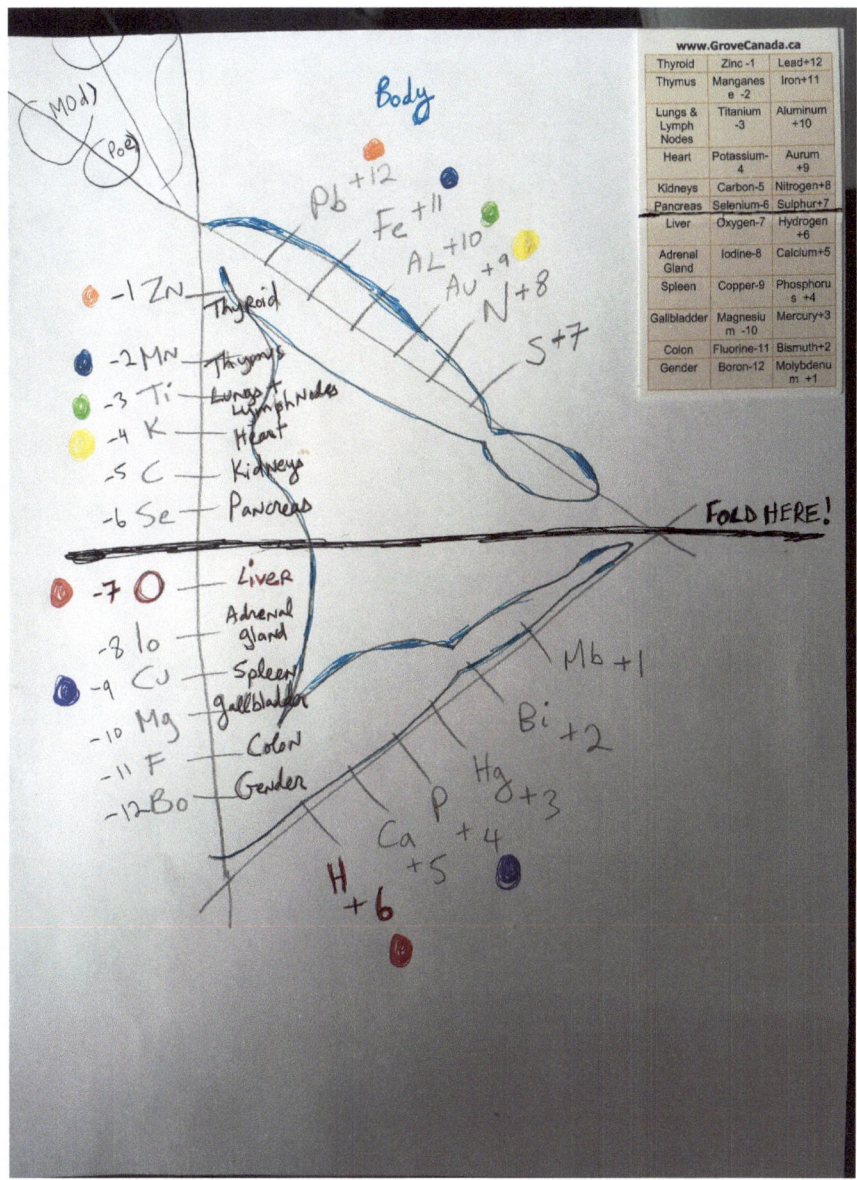

Body

Thyroid	Zinc -1	Lead+12
Thymus	Manganese -2	Iron+11
Lungs & Lymph Nodes	Titanium -3	Aluminum +10
Heart	Potassium-4	Aurum +9
Kidneys	Carbon-5	Nitrogen+8
Pancreas	Selenium-6	Sulphur+7
Liver	Oxygen-7	Hydrogen +6
Adrenal Gland	Iodine-8	Calcium+5
Spleen	Copper-9	Phosphorus +4
Gallbladder	Magnesium -10	Mercury+3
Colon	Fluorine-11	Bismuth+2
Gender	Boron-12	Molybdenum +1

Pb +12
Fe +11
AL +10
Au +9
N +8
S +7

-1 ZN — Thyroid
-2 MN — Thymus
-3 Ti — Lungs & Lymph Nodes
-4 K — Heart
-5 C — Kidneys
-6 Se — Pancreas

FOLD HERE!

-7 O — Liver
-8 Io — Adrenal gland
-9 Cu — Spleen
-10 Mg — Gallbladder
-11 F — Colon
-12 Bo — Gender

Mb +1
Bi +2
Hg +3
P +4
Ca +5
H +6

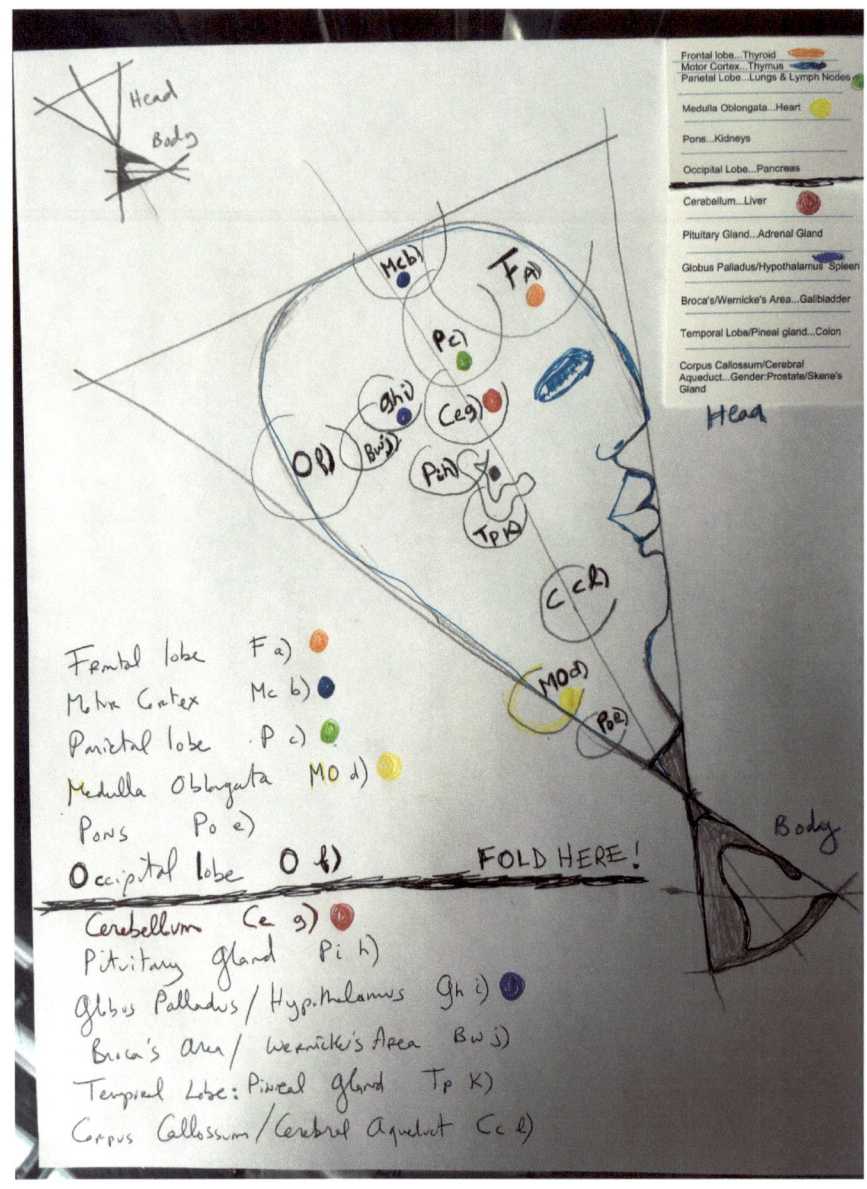

Frontal lobe…Thyroid
Motor Cortex…Thymus
Parietal Lobe…Lungs & Lymph Nodes

Medulla Oblongata…Heart

Pons…Kidneys

Occipital Lobe…Pancreas

Cerebellum…Liver

Pituitary Gland…Adrenal Gland

Globus Palladus/Hypothalamus Spleen

Broca's/Wernicke's Area…Gallbladder

Temporal Lobe/Pineal gland…Colon

Corpus Callossum/Cerebral
Aqueduct…Gender:Prostate/Skene's
Gland

Head

Body

Frontal lobe   F a)
Motor Cortex   Mc b)
Parietal lobe   . P c)
Medulla Oblongata   MO d)
Pons   Po e)
Occipital lobe   O f)   FOLD HERE!
Cerebellum   (Ce g)
Pituitary gland   Pi h)
Globus Palladus / Hyp.thalamus   Gh i)
Broca's area / Wernicke's Area   Bw j)
Temporal Lobe: Pineal gland   Tp K)
Corpus Callossum / Cerebral aqueduct   Cc l)

Toronto Area health Centres… Minus element for Women   Non-dominant Male element